TRUE STORY

Copyright © 2016 Scripture Union
First published 2016
ISBN 978 1 78506 520 0

Scripture Union England & Wales
207–209 Queensway, Bletchley,
Milton Keynes, MK2 2EB
info@scriptureunion.org.uk
www.scriptureunion.org.uk

British Library Cataloguing-in-Publication
Data: a catalogue record for this book is
available from the British Library.

The right of Pete Brown to be identified as author of
this work has been asserted by him in accordance
with the Copyright, Designs and Patents Act 1988.

Printed and bound in India by Nutech Print Services.

Designed by Luther Spicer

Scripture Union is an international Christian charity
working with churches in more than 130 countries.

Thank you for purchasing this book. Any profits
from this book support SU in England and Wales
to bring the good news of Jesus Christ to children,
young people and families and to enable them
to meet God through the Bible and prayer.

Find out more about our work and
how you can get involved at:

www.scriptureunion.org.uk (England and Wales)
www.suscotland.org.uk (Scotland)
www.suni.co.uk (Northern Ireland)
www.scriptureunion.org (USA)
www.su.org.au (Australia)

CONTENTS

I loved maths lessons at school. Firstly, my locker was located in the maths classroom and was a great place to store things that you really weren't supposed to be eating during lessons. And, secondly, there was underfloor heating. If all else failed, and the lesson was dragging on, you could take your shoes off, put your feet on the carpet tiles and with a bit of imagination it was like you were warming your feet by an open fire.

The main reason I loved maths lessons, though, was the many ways that we tried to flirt with the girls at the table on the opposite side of the room. It was easy enough to get their attention - a calculator and the sunlight that streamed into the classroom through the glass panels in the ceiling was all that was required.

Looking back, I'm not sure why we thought that trying to blind the objects of our affection by reflecting light into their eyes was a good idea, but it seemed so at the time. Yes, strange things happen at school.

At my school it was simply that the strange things always seemed to happen during maths. Like this one time Dean completely lost it with the teacher, kicked over his chair, pushed the table over and ran all the way home. He lived miles away too!

One thing is certain: these are not the stories to tell your parents, especially when the inevitable, **'How was school today?'** question comes up.

Just how are you supposed to answer that question anyway?

'Good, thanks. Dean had a minor meltdown and completely disrupted maths.' They'd only worry.

'Great, thanks. The girls in maths actually talked to us today.' But what if they brought it up at parents evening?

'Well, I had this amazing daydream about warming my feet by an open fire.' They'd never understand.

So instead, **'How was school today?'** **'Fine, thanks. It was... fine.'**

There are, of course, many important lessons to learn in school, aren't there? Many things we need to learn and understand. But, for me, the most important lesson I learnt at school was one that didn't feature in the National Curriculum. Because it was during my time at secondary school that I became a Christian. It was this, more than anything else, that was by far the most important thing that happened at school. Becoming a Christian totally transformed my life and helped me see what life is really all about.

So, thankfully, this book is not about maths lessons. After all, with the limited amount of actual maths that was done in my maths lessons at school, I'm not sure I'd be very qualified to speak about that. This book is about something far more important.

Over the pages that follow there will be more reflections from life at school but, more importantly, there will also be a chance to look at the evidence for Christianity for yourself. This has changed my life and it can change yours too. We'll also be dealing with some of the big questions people have about life, God, the universe and everything along the way.

My hope is that I will get you to start thinking about your life. What is it all about? What is it for?

In history you will have learnt about the Middle Ages, great kings and queens, and about wars that have been won and lost. Yet, have you ever thought about why the one whose birth we base the calendar of our human history upon, and the reason for holidays such as Christmas and Easter, doesn't seem to feature very much?

In English we learn about important literary works of the past and spend hours engaging with people who wrote plays, like Shakespeare, or important poems, like Wordsworth, Blake and Keats. Why is it, though, that the greatest literary work of all time, the world's best seller by a huge margin and the book upon which much of our society was built, is now often considered an irrelevance?

Maybe, just maybe, there is one subject we have overlooked – the subject of God and the meaning of our lives. That is what this book is all about. I hope you enjoy it!

Each chapter of this book is based around an encounter with Jesus and the impact that he had on people's lives. Jesus Christ was born a little over 2,000 years ago. He was a man who claimed to be God. His story is recorded for us in four eyewitness accounts which are known as Gospels.

The word **'gospel'** means **'good news'**.

The four Gospels in the Bible are named after the people who wrote them – Matthew, Mark, Luke and John – and we'll be looking at parts of their stories throughout this book.

My aim for each chapter is a simple one – that in reading the Gospels for yourself you will meet the real Jesus. Not the Jesus that you may have pictured in your mind – you know the one, some bloke with long hair, blue eyes and sandals – but rather the Jesus whose life is recorded in the Bible. The Jesus of history. The Jesus who Christians believe still lives, still speaks and is still at work today.

BOOK...

In each chapter, after a short introduction, I'm going to ask you to read a passage from the Bible. These words are written either by people who knew Jesus personally or relied on the eyewitness accounts of those who did.

Before reading these bits from the Bible, why not say something to God like:

> **'God, I have no idea whether you exist or not. But if you do, I want to find out. I want to know whether you are really there and what you want to say to me.'**

Every chapter starts with a 'Big Question' to be thinking about – the sort of question that might pop into your head whilst you're supposed to be thinking about something else entirely.

After reading the Bible passage and thinking about the big question, I'd like you to reflect on what you've just read. Why not write some stuff down? In fact, scribble, doodle and write all over this book – that's exactly why it's been designed as it has! In each chapter there are some questions for you to think about. Then there is a short summary of what you've read to get you thinking further.

I hope by the time you reach the end of this book you will have started to understand more about what Christians believe and why many people have come to believe that God's story is the most amazing story of all. If you come to a point of deciding for yourself that this is true, there will be some suggestions about what to do about that.

IS THERE A GOD?

HISTORY

The first lesson I had at secondary school was history, with another Mr Brown. His first question to us was, 'Year 7, what is history?' Silence. It was our first lesson and no one wanted to look stupid.

'History,' said Mr Brown, 'is *his* story, *his story*, HISTORY!' He seemed very pleased with himself at this observation. Very pleased indeed.

I think he meant the story of mankind... but actually, in a different sense, I couldn't agree more.

How can we know there is a God? The central story of the Bible is that God himself was born into our world so that we might know that there is a God and also see for ourselves what he is like. History is his story.

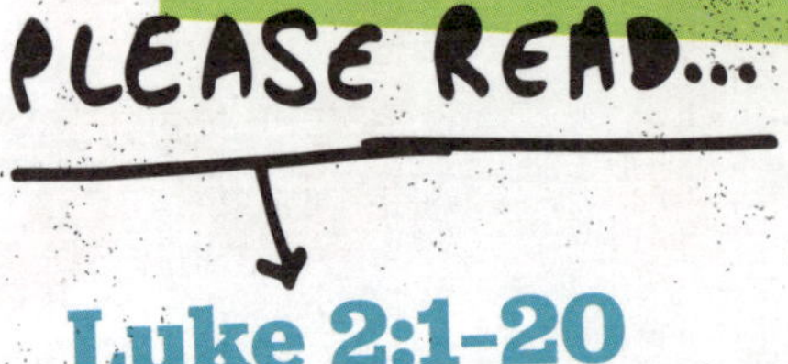

Every book of the Bible is divided into **chapters** and **verses**. Luke 2:1-20 means Luke chapter two and verses 1 to 20. The large numbers on the Bible pages are chapter numbers and the smaller numbers are verse numbers.

PLEASE READ...

Luke 2:1-20

These words are written by a man called Luke, a first-century doctor and historian. He researched carefully the events surrounding the birth of Jesus Christ and recorded them for us. As you read them, think about what evidence you can find that suggests to you that Luke wants us to treat this story as a historical document.

Luke 2:1-20

2 In those days Caesar Augustus issued a decree that a census should be taken of the entire Roman world. ² (This was the first census that took place while Quirinius was governor of Syria.) ³ And everyone went to their own town to register.

⁴ So Joseph also went up from the town of Nazareth in Galilee to Judea, to Bethlehem the town of David, because he belonged to the house and line of David. ⁵ He went there to register with Mary, who was pledged to be married to him and was expecting a child. ⁶ While they were there, the time came for the baby to be born, ⁷ and she gave birth to her firstborn, a son. She wrapped him in cloths and placed him in a manger, because there was no guest room available for them.

⁸ And there were shepherds living out in the fields near by, keeping watch over their flocks at night. ⁹ An angel of the Lord appeared to them, and the glory of the Lord shone around them, and they were terrified. ¹⁰ But the angel said to them, 'Do not be afraid. I bring you good news that will cause great joy for all the people. ¹¹ Today in the town of David a Saviour has been born to you; he is the Messiah,

the Lord. [12] This will be a sign to you: you will find a baby wrapped in cloths and lying in a manger.'

[13] Suddenly a great company of the heavenly host appeared with the angel, praising God and saying,

[14] 'Glory to God in the highest heaven, and on earth peace to those on whom his favour rests.'

[15] When the angels had left them and gone into heaven, the shepherds said to one another, 'Let's go to Bethlehem and see this thing that has happened, which the Lord has told us about.'

[16] So they hurried off and found Mary and Joseph, and the baby, who was lying in the manger. [17] When they had seen him, they spread the word concerning what had been told them about this child, [18] and all who heard it were amazed at what the shepherds said to them. [19] But Mary treasured up all these things and pondered them in her heart. [20] The shepherds returned, glorifying and praising God for all the things they had heard and seen, which were just as they had been told.

Now that you have read about the first people who met
Jesus, have a think about the following questions. All
the answers can be found in the Bible passage.

PAUSE + THINK...

When did the birth of Jesus happen?

How many witnesses were there to Jesus being born?

What do the angels say about who Jesus is?

What evidence are we given that God exists?

**If you could interview one person from
this story, who would it be and why?**

Roman history

Everyone learns about the Romans at school, don't they? Roman roads, Hadrian's Wall and even the odd terrible joke from your history teacher – 'Did you know that the Romans divided Gaul into three parts? Apparently, they used a pair of Caesars.' (OK, OK, no more jokes, I promise.)

Caesar Augustus was the adopted son of Julius Caesar and became emperor of Rome following the assassination of his great uncle in 44 BC. He decided one day that his dead adoptive father was divine and so referred to himself as a 'son of god'. Small ego that man, don't you think?

Luke tells us that Jesus was born at the time of Caesar Augustus so that we would know he is writing real history. At the same time as Caesar has decided for himself that he is god, another man is born who will be known as the true Son of God.

Today, 21 centuries later, no one takes Caesar Augustus' claim to be god seriously. But I know lots of people who still believe that Jesus Christ is the Son of God.

Luke tells us that Mary and Joseph travelled to Bethlehem to register for a census. Caesar didn't want to miss out on any of the taxes people owed because, after all, it was almost certainly expensive trying to live like a god. It is while they were in Bethlehem that Mary gave birth to Jesus.

Some people today think that Jesus was a mythical figure who never actually existed, but hardly any serious historians would agree. Instead, the best evidence we have shows us that Jesus was definitely born and lived at this time in history.

Angel flash mob

When I was born I think my mum and dad phoned a few friends and family to tell them the news. As far as I know there were no angels. In fact I've not heard of another birth that has ever been announced by first one and then a whole flash mob of angels.

What they said is really important:

'I bring you good news that will cause great joy for all the people.'

I wonder what your opinion of Christianity is? If you know any Christians, what words would you use to describe them? The Christians that I knew at secondary school seemed to be genuinely joyful. I figured that either they were just really weird or they must know something that I didn't.

But, it's the second thing that the angels say that is possibly most important:

'Today in the town of David a Saviour has been born to you; he is the Messiah, the Lord.'

Bethlehem, where Jesus was born, was also known as the town of David. The angels tell the shepherds that it is here that God himself had been born into the world. If we had been alive at the time of Jesus we could have seen God with our own eyes. He was born into human history.

The angels also say why God was born. He didn't come as a teacher to educate us, or as a magician to do tricks for us, but as a Saviour to save us.

What does this mean for us?

'Glory to God in the highest heaven, and on earth peace to those on whom his favour rests.'

I used to worry about a lot of things when I was growing up. My dad would often say, 'Cross that bridge when you come to it.' It was his way of reminding me not to worry about things that might never happen.

But sometimes bad things do happen in our lives and in our world, don't they? Peace on earth, or even in our lives, seems like something we could only ever dream of.

Maybe you know people at school who worry about exams, about friends, about their appearance... Maybe you are even concerned about some of these things yourself.

Jesus was born so that we can have peace - peace with God and real peace in our lives. He came to show us that there is a God who loves us, who is interested in us and who

was born on earth for us. Jesus can show us what God is really like and he can give us peace.

Sometimes people tell me that Christianity is boring, irrelevant and untrue. I hope that in reading this first Bible passage for yourself you're prepared to question that.

Is Jesus' birth boring? It's not exactly the sort of birth that happens every day, is it?

As for being untrue, Luke goes out of his way to point out that he's writing real history, that we should treat his Gospel in the same way as other historical documents.

Finally, the angels say that far from being irrelevant, the story of Jesus is actually good news for us all. Not just for the people then, but for us today. Why? Because not only is there a God, he is a God who can give meaning to our lives as his story starts to impact our story.

WHAT DO YOU THINK?

Why do/don't you believe in God?

What is your impression of what Christians are like?

What question(s) would you like to ask God?

Kristina's story

I believe in God because I don't think
that this world could be an accident.
There is so much beauty, detail and
variety which tells us something
about what God must be like.

WHAT IS GOD LIKE?

PSHE

I think it's a general rule that there are some subjects at school that are seen as less important than others. I remember many of my teachers from school but I'll admit that I haven't got a clue who taught us PSHE. In fact, I'm not sure I ever really had a clue what PSHE was all about.

But I do remember one PSHE lesson very clearly. The one with the supply teacher.

Looking back, we must have been extremely gullible, but at the time it seemed like such a good idea. Someone had heard that if different members of the class started humming very quietly at different times the teacher wouldn't be able to tell who was humming. This would mean we could avoid working through whatever text book we had been given to read and have a joke at the supply teacher's expense. Of course, because they were a supply teacher they wouldn't be able to do anything about it.

It was entertaining for all of about a minute. One person started humming, then another person started humming. Soon the whole room was humming along together. And, although it was only meant to be a bit of fun, the whole class immediately received a lunchtime detention.

I think lots of people think that if there is a God, he's probably a bit like our supply teacher – either waiting to hand out detentions to stop us having fun and/or not able to do very much about anything at all.

In this chapter we're going to look at another account from Luke's Gospel. About 30 years after his birth, Jesus wasn't teaching PSHE, but he was talking about one lesson in life that is of ultimate importance. He wants us to think about the meaning of life and what God is truly like.

PLEASE READ...

Luke 15:1,2,11-24

Luke 15:1,2,11-24

15 *Now the tax collectors and sinners were all gathering round to hear Jesus.* ^{2} *But the Pharisees and the teachers of the law muttered, 'This man welcomes sinners, and eats with them.'*

^{11} *Jesus continued: 'There was a man who had two sons.* ^{12} *The younger one said to his father, "Father, give me my share of the estate." So he divided his property between them.*

^{13} *'Not long after that, the younger son got together all he had, set off for a distant country and there squandered his wealth in wild living.* ^{14} *After he had spent everything, there was a severe famine in that whole country, and he began to be in need.* ^{15} *So he went and hired himself out to a citizen of that country, who sent him to his fields to feed pigs.* ^{16} *He longed to fill his stomach with the pods that the pigs were eating, but no one gave him anything.*

^{17} *'When he came to his senses, he said, "How many of my father's hired servants have food to spare, and here I am starving to death!* ^{18} *I will set out and go back to my father and say to him: Father, I have sinned against heaven and against you.* ^{19} *I am no longer worthy to be called your son; make me like one of your hired servants."* ^{20} *So he got up and went to his father.*

'But while he was still a long way off, his father saw him and was filled with compassion for him; he ran to his son, threw his arms round him and kissed him.

^{21} *'The son said to him, "Father, I have sinned against heaven and against you. I am no longer worthy to be called your son."*

[22] 'But the father said to his servants, "Quick! Bring the best robe and put it on him. Put a ring on his finger and sandals on his feet. [23] Bring the fattened calf and kill it. Let's have a feast and celebrate. [24] For this son of mine was dead and is alive again; he was lost and is found." So they began to celebrate.'

PAUSE + THINK...

**Why are people moaning about Jesus
at the beginning of the passage?**

**How do you think your family would respond if
you asked for your share of your inheritance?**

**What is surprising about how the father
responds when his son comes home?**

**The father in Jesus' story represents God.
What do we learn about what God is like?**

If it makes you happy

Some people dream of leaving school with as many A* grades as they can. Some just dream of leaving. Some dream of earning as much money as they can and others dream of making a difference. Does it matter what our dream in life is? Surely as long as it makes you happy, that's the main thing?

The younger son in the Bible passage had a dream. He knew what life was all about - he didn't need PSHE lessons. It was about leaving home and living a life filled with money and as many parties as possible. There was just one problem: his father.

His dad was - how do I put this? - a bit of an inconvenience. As long as the son lived at home he had to do what his father said. And while his father was alive the son wasn't going to have as much money as he needed to be happy.

So he asked his dad to give him his inheritance - his share of what he would receive when his father died. 'Dad, I wish you were dead so I could have your money now.' That's pretty offensive, isn't it?

It's more than slightly surprising, therefore, that his dad gives him exactly what he asks for.

For a while, his life was indeed much better. This son lived the life that he had dreamed about. Money, parties, fast camels... everything he had set his heart upon.

Until the money ran out. And a famine came. And he ended up in a job nobody else would do, dreaming of eating the food that he was feeding to the pigs. The dream had turned into a nightmare.

Actually though, as so often with the stories that Jesus told, this story isn't just about one son. Jesus wants us to see that this story is about every human being who has ever lived. It's my story and it's yours.

The father in this story represents God.

There must be more

The Bible tells us that far from being like a grumpy supply teacher, God is more like a loving and generous father. He gives all of us many good things - our world, our lives and, ultimately, every good thing we enjoy.

Yet, often, we find ourselves wanting the good things in life but want nothing to do with the Giver - just like the younger son. Many people even end up thinking life is all about the good things, and about grabbing as many of the good things as we can get our hands on!

Life would be better if only we...

had more money,

had more friends,

had a better mobile phone,

had better grades.

Many of these things will make life better, but never as much as we imagine they will. The friendship or relationship that we wanted isn't as fulfilling as we'd hoped - so we look for another one. The mobile phone is replaced by a newer model - so we dream of a better one.

Many are left wondering, surely there must be more to life than all of this? And that's because there is.

The son in our story started daydreaming about his former life at home. He reasoned that even the people who worked for his father had a better life than him. Maybe he could make things up with his dad. Maybe he could pay off his debts. There was only one thing for it: he'd have to go home.

But, while he was far off, his dad saw him and ran towards him.

Now, at this point in the story you might be thinking... the son is in for it now - he's going to be grounded for life/punished in some horrible and painful way.

But, shockingly, his dad didn't even let him finish the speech he had planned. Instead he throws his arms around him and organises a huge party to celebrate. For the son who was lost had been found.

We see in this story a father who is desperate to welcome his son home. This is what God is like.

Amazing grace

Sometimes people think that God just wants to spoil our fun, to cramp our style. In fact, nothing could be further from the truth. For it is only when we come to know God for ourselves, only in relationship with him, that we find what life is truly all about. The Bible tells us that the good material things that come from God cannot ultimately satisfy us – only a relationship with God can do that.

But more than anything else, this story teaches us something massively important about God: he is a God who gives what we don't deserve. Christians often call this grace.

At school your work will often be graded according to your performance. God is not like that. Instead he freely offers everyone what they don't deserve – his love, welcome and forgiveness. Grace is when God gives us things we don't deserve – the relationship we were created for.

In our story, the father didn't tell his son he had to clean up his act and sort himself out before he could come home. No, he just said **'Come home. Come just as you are.'**

God gives the same invitation to every one of us.

For me, this was one of the most striking things about the Christian faith. In every other religion, as far as I could tell, it was all about me doing things to somehow make myself acceptable to God. But Christianity was different. There was a God who loved me and wanted to know me, just as I was. A God who was prepared to offer me exactly what I didn't deserve: forgiveness from past mistakes, love, acceptance and security. All I had to do was to turn back to him.

WHAT DO YOU THINK?

What are your hopes and fears in life?

How has reading this chapter changed your understanding of what God is like?

How does it feel to hear that God is interested in your life?

Louis' story

If someone lived, died and came back
to life again, we are left with no other
option than to accept his claim to be
God. All other options are off the table.

IS JESUS REALLY GOD?

PHYSICS

Physics lessons at my school had one general rule: practical lessons exciting; theory lessons dull. Partly this was due to the fact that Mr Smith, our science teacher, always seemed to get just a little bit too excited by these practical experiments. Surely, there is a limit to how excited one man can get when you do the same experiments every year? He particularly loved the one with the electric ball thing that makes your hair stand on end. Have you tried that one?

We read in the first chapter about the birth of Jesus Christ. It was an unusual birth, I think you'll agree. However, the proof of this claim that he was God would surely be seen as he grew up. That is what we see in this next account, as Jesus gives us evidence to back up the angels' claim. I can't even begin to imagine what Mr Smith would have made of this account of Jesus.

PLEASE READ...

Mark 6:45-51

This is the sort of science practical that would never pass health and safety regulations, isn't it! I'm sure even Mr Smith would not have been able to get this one past our headmaster, although I could definitely imagine him trying. **'Yes, headmaster, that's right, I want to take the pupils into the middle of a large lake, during a really violent storm, and see if, given the right conditions, they can walk on the water. So exciting, don't you think?'**

What do you think about what you've just read?

PAUSE + THINK...

Where does this story about Jesus happen?

How do Jesus' actions support the claim that he was God?

What reactions do we see from Jesus' disciples?

Do you think this is what they were expecting? Why/why not?

Don't try this at home

Jesus' disciples are in a spot of bother. They're stuck in the middle of large lake, at night and a storm is coming. However, we're told that Jesus had seen them. He'd seen them struggling to keep their boat afloat.

Something is about to happen. Mr Smith would have been doing a little bit of bouncing up and down at this point.

'Shortly before dawn he [Jesus] went out to them, walking on the lake.'

I'm sorry, did you miss that? He went for a casual stroll... on a lake.

This is your classic health warning stuff: don't try this at home. Or at least, if you do, make sure you're in the bath and not in the middle of a lake.

But here is Jesus and he's walking on the lake. You know, as you do!

It's not surprising that the disciples are terrified. People don't walk on water. Not then. Not now. Except that Jesus really did. And, as he does so, he speaks to them.

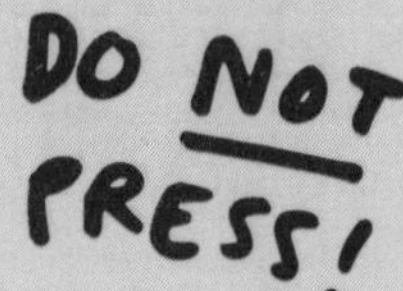

"I AM"

I AM

This part of the Bible was originally written in Greek and a more literal translation of what he says here would be, 'Take courage, I AM.' Although it's not very good English, it's helpful as we think about what Jesus is saying here.

You could be forgiven for thinking, I am... what? I am... terrifying you at this precise moment in time? I am... not behaving in a very normal way?

But what Jesus is actually doing is describing himself using the same words that God used to refer to himself in the first half of the Bible, which we call the Old Testament.

He says to them, **'Take courage, because I AM... God. The reason I can walk on the lake is because I am God. So don't be afraid. You're not going to drown.'**

Watch and learn

I've always wondered, though, why it is that Jesus walks out on the water to them. I mean, he didn't need to, did he? He could have had a quiet word with the wind and the waves from where he was. In fact, if you've ever read the whole of Mark's Gospel then you'll know he's already done something like that before. (In Mark 4:35–41 Jesus calmed a storm.)

But here he wants his friends to learn something important. He wants them to see that his miracles reveal something about who he is and about what he expects.

The way someone walks often tells us something about them, doesn't it? The headmaster of our school had the walk of a man with authority. He also happened to be very good at chess. The school bully walked with the swagger of someone who, by some freak of nature, must have been almost 6 feet tall in Year 7!

Jesus walked on a lake. The middle of a lake that was 8 miles wide.

When we saw Mr Smith using his Van de Graaff Generator (yes, yes, OK, I admit it, I did just google what his electric ball thing was called) we were amazed and a little bit entertained. But Jesus is not looking for us to be amazed. He didn't want his disciples to be entertained. He's looking for something else. He is looking for people to look at what he does and listen to what he says. He is looking for something the Bible calls 'faith'.

A Christian is someone who has looked at the evidence and come to believe for themselves that Jesus really is who he said he was. The words that he spoke, the miracles that he performed, the perfect life he led all point to the fact that he is God.

But so what? Why should that make any difference to life today? Why should I bother with God? We'll think about that next.

WHAT DO YOU THINK?

What would someone need to do to prove to you that they were God?

Why do/don't you believe the miracles that Jesus did?

After reading this chapter, how would you finish this sentence: 'A Christian is someone who...'?

Dan's story

I love being a Christian because I know that I will never be alone, because the God of everything loves me and wants to spend time with me. I think it's incredible that anyone can talk to God whenever they want, about whatever they want, knowing that God will listen. I also know that when I face difficult times, I have someone to talk to, who can make a difference.

WHY DO I NEED TO BOTHER WITH GOD?

BIOLOGY

To try and lighten the mood, or maybe to prevent himself from passing out, one of my classmates decided to make use of his remote control wristwatch, which also happened to work the video player. The teacher pressed play on the machine; Chris pressed pause on his watch. The teacher pressed play on the machine; Chris turned the volume up to full. The teacher, flustered by now, told us not to worry and left the classroom to find a technician. We all got a break.

I think everyone was thinking, *do we really need to do bother with this?*

Some people ask the same question when it comes to God. Why do I need to bother with God? So what if there is a God? So what if he came to earth as Jesus? Why should I care? This next passage from Mark's Gospel will get us thinking about that question.

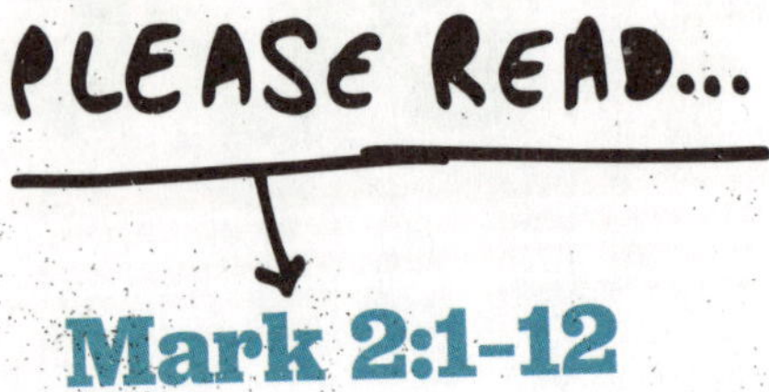

Mark 2:1-12

This account of a man who couldn't walk is even more memorable than our school lesson on human reproduction. What do you make of it?

PAUSE + THINK...

Why do you think the friends were bringing the paralysed man to Jesus?

What words would you use to describe the paralysed man's friends?

Jesus immediately wants to help this man with his biggest problem. But what does Jesus think that is?

Why does this infuriate the religious leaders so much?

How did Jesus prove that he was able to forgive the man?

How did people respond when they saw this happen? How do you think you would have responded?

Through the roof

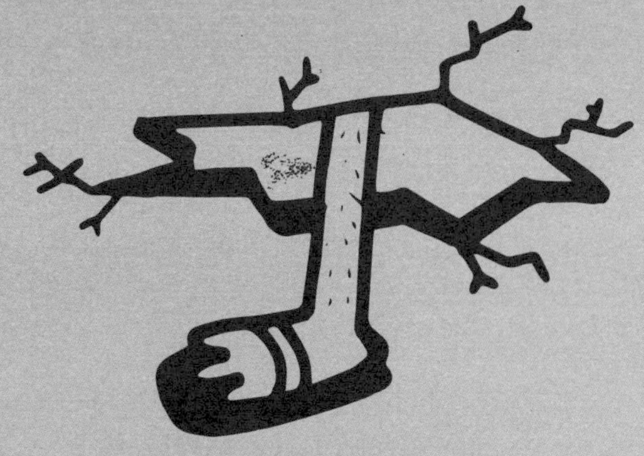

Getting to see Jesus was a bit like trying to get a ticket to Glastonbury - it required commitment.

However, the friends in our story decided that not having a ticket for this particular gig didn't need to be a problem for them. They would just go in through the roof!

I'm not sure how you'd feel if someone broke in through the roof of your house. It would probably result in a swift call to the police! But these men were desperate to see Jesus because they'd heard what people were saying - Jesus can heal people!

Their mate was paralysed so you can understand their desperation. They were thinking that maybe Jesus could heal him too. So they made a hole in the roof and lowered him down on a mat.

All eyes must have been on Jesus as he looked at the man and said,

'Son, your sins are forgiven.'

I think there were probably embarrassed whispers. **'Umm, Jesus, that's not exactly what they were hoping for.'** Because everyone thought they knew what this man's biggest need was.

Prove it

To make matters worse, the religious leaders of the day accused Jesus of blasphemy - that is, of disrespecting God. They knew that only God can forgive people. And they weren't ready to believe that he really was God.

But Jesus knew what they were thinking and so he said,

'Which is easier: to say to this paralysed man, "Your sins are forgiven," or to say, "Get up, take your mat and walk"?'

This is one of those questions that some teachers insist on asking at school. The sort of question that everyone knows the answer to but no one is prepared to answer because it's just far too obvious.

Of course it's easier to say your sins are forgiven, because no one can tell if that has actually happened or not. Anyone could go around saying that. Where's the proof?

'Here's the proof,' said Jesus. **'Get up and walk!'**

And the man did. Which, you have to admit, is staggering. Jesus is saying our greatest need is to be forgiven. That was even more important for this man than whether he could walk.

Consequences

If you're going to understand why Jesus says we all need to be forgiven, then you need to understand sin.

Think for a moment about what happens when your teacher leaves the classroom. They'll probably say something like, 'Please continue working through exercise three, in silence, until I return.'

What happens next? The noise levels rise, mobile phones appear and all sorts of chaos breaks out.

The teacher's instructions are rarely obeyed when the teacher is out of the room. Sin is like that, it's just that it's God we're disobeying and not a teacher. Because we can't see God with our eyes we live as though he's not there and ignore his standards.

If we're honest with ourselves, we know we don't always live up to our own standards or the rules our school has, let alone the standards of a perfect God.

Ultimately, sin is a rejection of God. This happens in many different ways:

- Denying God – I don't believe you exist

- Disobeying God – I know you exist but I don't want to live according to your rules

- Acting like I am God – whether or not you exist, I want to do things my way

But why is treating God like this such a serious problem?

If you ignore a teacher, sometimes you will get away with it but at other times the whole class might be given a detention. We might not like it very much, but at school, the teacher is in charge. They get to decide what an appropriate consequence looks like.

It's a bit like that with God. If we break God's rules, there's also a consequence to our actions.

We miss out on the relationship that we were created to enjoy. Like the younger son in chapter 2, we forget that God created us, loves us, knows us better than anyone else and wants what is best for us. When we reject God, we miss out on all the good things that he has for us.

Then, at the end of our lives, we face the prospect of being eternally separated from God in a place that Jesus says is to be avoided at all costs. If we reject God then we face being cut off from the life, joy and happiness that God created us to enjoy for eternity.

Sick

Sometimes in life the biggest problems are the ones that you need someone else to tell you about. If a doctor tells you that you are sick then you'll probably listen and take the medicine you are given.

God tells us our biggest problem in life is not a physical sickness but a spiritual sickness – the Bible calls this sin. Yet it is because of his great love for us that God sent Jesus to be the Saviour we need, to take the punishment our sins deserve and to offer us forgiveness.

When we think, *I'm quite alright without God, thank you very much,* it is because we don't see that our greatest need is forgiveness. We think what we need most is more money, a newer mobile phone, more friends, better exam results.

Jesus says that what we need most is forgiveness, so that we can enjoy the life God wants for us now and, one day, be with him in heaven. That is what the next chapter is all about.

WHAT DO YOU THINK?

When was the last time you felt the need for forgiveness?

What problems would you ask God to help you with?

Why do you think someone should/
shouldn't be interested in God?

Chloe's story

One of the most important promises in the Bible is that this life is not all there is. The certain hope that I have of eternal life helps me to think about this life in a completely different way.

IS THERE LIFE AFTER DEATH?

a + x = BORED
MATHS

I loved maths lessons at school. My mum was a maths teacher, which meant that any homework was always a doddle for her... umm, I mean for me... when I did it all completely by myself.

The thing I loved most about maths was that there was always a right answer. It wasn't like English where everything was a matter of opinion. Maths was logical, dependable and strangely reassuring.

The question for this chapter is a huge one: is there life after death? It's a pretty important question, don't you think? I realise that thinking about death, which is probably a long way off, isn't something you do every day. But surely it's a logical question to think about? There must be a right answer. Is there life after death or not?

In our next passage from Luke's Gospel, Jesus is being led out to die on a cross. As he faces his own death, he assures another man that eternity is a reality.

PLEASE READ...

Luke 23:32-49

We're supposed to read this account and think: it doesn't seem fair, does it? Two men are being punished for crimes that carried the death penalty. Jesus is being punished for... well, what exactly?

What do you think?

PAUSE + THINK...

Jesus has just been nailed to a cross. What is surprising about the first words that he speaks?

How would you describe the different reactions of the people who watch Jesus die?

What is different about how the second criminal speaks to Jesus?

What promise does Jesus make to this second criminal and what do you think he means?

If you could have asked Jesus one question as he hung on the cross, what would it have been?

It wasn't me!

During one maths lesson, Steve, who sat next to me and was obviously bored, decided to start throwing the base ten cubes we were using that lesson at people on the opposite side of the classroom. Somehow, our teacher who was writing on the whiteboard at the time didn't notice.

Things got slightly out of hand, however, when a thousand cube was catapulted, via ruler, into an overhead light. Everyone noticed that. But our teacher was convinced that it was my other friend Rob who had launched the cube. I don't think I've ever heard someone complain so loudly at the injustice – as he took the punishment Steve deserved.

In the account we've just read, one of the most striking things is that as he was dying on the cross, Jesus wasn't protesting his innocence, or shouting abuse at those who had nailed him there. This is in spite of the fact that the people who were standing around were mocking him.

To us, death often comes as a cruel shock. We sometimes say that someone was taken away from us before their time or that they were too young to die. The startling thing with the death of Jesus, however, is that he had actually been predicting his own death for a long time. He seemed to know how he would die, when he would die and why he would die.

On one occasion Jesus, who often referred to himself as the 'Son of Man', said,

'We are going up to Jerusalem, and the Son of Man will be delivered over to the chief priests and the teachers of the law. They will condemn him to death and will hand him over to the Gentiles to be mocked and flogged and crucified. On the third day he will be raised to life!'

(Matthew 20:18,19)

Rebel, rebel

The question we're meant to have as we read Luke's story of the crucifixion is this: why is Jesus being crucified like a common criminal? Why is Jesus dying the death of a rebel?

The answer the Bible gives is staggering. He is dying the death of a rebel because he is dying in the place of rebels. Some people like to think that their good deeds will somehow make up for their bad ones. The Bible tells us this isn't how it works.

Instead, Jesus, who had done nothing wrong, is dying so that we can have life after death. Because God doesn't want anyone to be separated from him eternally.

On the cross Jesus turns to the second criminal and says, **'Today you will be with me in paradise.'**

The Bible says that we will all spend eternity somewhere. The only question is: where?

Remember that when Jesus was born the angels said,

'Today in the town of David a Saviour has been born to you; he is the Messiah, the Lord.'

It is here on the cross that Jesus accomplished his mission of saving people from their sin. Nobody wants to die; in fact most people do as much as they can to live as long as they can. But we all know that one day we will die. But because of Jesus there is now the possibility of life with God even after death.

In one of the most famous verses in the whole of the Bible we read,

'For God so loved the world that he gave his one and only Son, that whoever believes in him shall not perish but have eternal life.' (John 3:16)

The truth, whether we realise it or not, is that we have all thought, said and done things that deserve God's punishment. What we deserve is to be cut off from him for ever. But when he died on the cross, Jesus was paying the penalty for our sins. He was dying in our place. Jesus volunteers to take that punishment on our behalf to save us.

This is what the second criminal who hung on the cross that day came to realise. Jesus was dying for him so that even someone like him could be forgiven and receive eternal life. He knew there was nothing he could do to earn this himself. So he simply trusted Jesus and said,

'Remember me when you come into your kingdom.'

Faith

I don't know if you've noticed, but Christians talk a lot about faith, don't they? The importance of faith in Jesus. This thief helps us to see what faith is all about.

First, faith requires a change of heart – we sometimes call this repentance. Repentance simply means a total change of direction. This thief doesn't join in with everyone else abusing Jesus, instead he realises that he is getting what he deserves. On the cross he turns away from his past and he turns to Jesus.

Secondly, faith required this thief to believe that Jesus could do something about his situation. Faith, at its heart, means taking Jesus at his word and trusting that he is able to keep it. He realised that Jesus was able to give him life, even after death. Soon afterwards this man would take his last breath in this life... and his first breath in heaven.

The certain hope that Christians have is a real physical life after death with God in heaven. A life that is even more physical and real than the one we are currently living. We might think that death is the end. Jesus says that because of his death, it can be the doorway to eternal life.

The proof Jesus will offer, that this is really true, is his own resurrection. That is what our next chapter is all about.

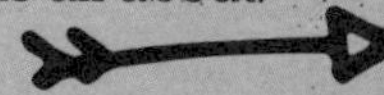

WHAT DO YOU THINK?

What do you think happens after people die?

**What would you want to say to someone
who had just died to save you?**

Why do/don't you believe in life after death?

Ben's story

To me, the evidence, both historical and personal, is irrefutable. Jesus must be God! Jesus has made a greater impact on history than anyone else. When I look at all God has done for me in this life, any doubt of his existence is gone.

HOW DO i KNOW THIS IS TRUE?

ENGLISH

Everyone reads a bit of Shakespeare at school, don't they? Or at least you need to pretend you've read a little Shakespeare when in fact you've just watched the film version instead. (Everyone still does that, don't they?)

Shakespeare was one of the greatest writers we have ever had. Unless you believed a girl in my class called Sarah. Sarah's mum had told her that Shakespeare actually got someone else to write his plays. I don't think anyone ever took her seriously.

However, some people do take this issue seriously. Mark Twain, another famous author, once wrote, 'So far as anybody actually knows and can prove, Shakespeare of Stratford-on-Avon never wrote a play in his life.'

I have to admit I wasn't that fussed about who wrote Shakespeare. Somebody did and we were going to be examined on it.

When it comes to Christianity, however, the question, **'How do we know any of this is actually true?'** seemed far more important to me.

The Bible says it all stands or falls on one event: the resurrection of Jesus Christ.

Resurrection means coming back to life after death.

So let's take a look. This is John's account of events.

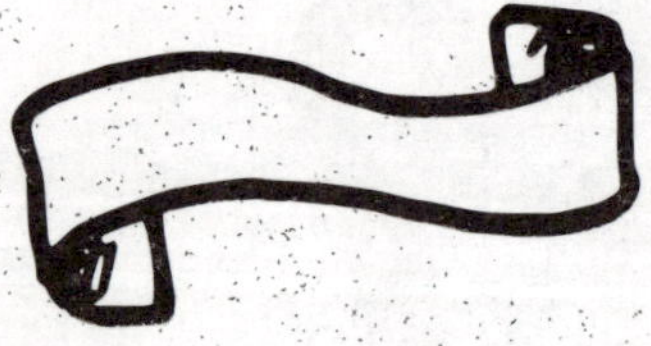

PLEASE READ...

John 20:1-29

If Jesus is simply a famous person from history, like Shakespeare, then we can probably safely ignore him, or watch a film version of his life sometime. But if he really rose from the dead I think this changes things slightly, don't you?

Because dead people don't tend to come back to life. Dead people stay dead. It's just that Jesus didn't. And hundreds of people at the time said they saw him alive. And millions of people since believe that he is alive today. Are they all completely mad? Or could there be something to this?

Have a think for yourself about the following questions.

PAUSE + THINK...

What do you think Mary Magdalene was expecting to find when she went to the tomb?

How do you think she felt when she realised he was alive?

Why do you think Jesus asks his disciples to look at his hands and his side?

How could the authorities have tried to prove that Jesus was still dead?

Why didn't Thomas believe that Jesus was alive?

Jesus said, 'Because you have seen me, you have believed; blessed are those who have not seen and yet have believed.' What do you think he meant?

Conspiracy theories

There is very good evidence that Shakespeare did, in fact, write his plays. Not everyone is prepared to believe this evidence, of course. Some people will believe whatever they want to believe. Apparently some people today still believe the moon landing was just a big conspiracy and it was all filmed in a studio.

But I don't get the impression that the resurrection of Jesus was just a big conspiracy, do you?

It doesn't seem to me like the people just really wanted Jesus to be alive and believed in spite of all the evidence. In fact, it seems in the passage you've just read as though everyone was expecting him to be dead.

Mary went to the tomb in order to pour perfume on Jesus' dead body. They didn't bury people underground in Jesus' day and so perfume was necessary to hide the smell. Her first reaction was that Jesus' body had been stolen.

When Peter and the other disciple (probably John who wrote these words) ran to the tomb and found it empty they didn't have a clue that Jesus had to rise from the dead.

Next we hear how Mary was so distressed that through her tears she mistook Jesus for a gardener.

Finally, Thomas, who wasn't with the rest of the disciples when Jesus appeared to them, refused to believe that they weren't all just making it up. He said,

'Unless I see the nail marks in his hands and put my finger where the nails were, and put my hand into his side, I will not believe.'

Fact or fiction?

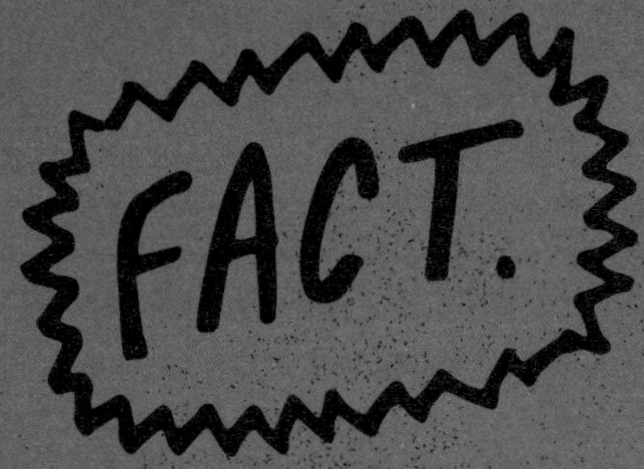

Over the years many people have come up with theories as to why the resurrection of Jesus Christ didn't happen.

Maybe the body was stolen. But if the body had been stolen then surely a rotting corpse would have been produced to put an end once and for all to this strange claim that Jesus had risen?

Maybe the disciples were hallucinating because they couldn't cope with the fact that Jesus had been killed. But on one occasion Jesus appeared to over 500 people at once. It seems a bit of a stretch to imagine that they all had the same hallucination at once.

Maybe the disciples stole the body and it was all a big conspiracy. Yet the tomb was guarded by Roman soldiers to prevent just this sort of thing happening. Then, later, most of Jesus' closest followers would be put to death for saying the resurrection truly happened. And not one them, even when on trial for their lives, admitted to making it all up.

The tomb was empty. There was no body. Jesus appeared to multiple people on many occasions over several weeks. And Christianity exploded on to the scene of history. Thousands of people began worshipping Jesus quite literally overnight. Today there are millions and millions of Christians in our world.

At the end of our story Jesus appeared to Thomas, the one who had doubted it all, and when Thomas saw Jesus he said to him, **'My Lord and my God!'**

At this moment Jesus doesn't say, **'Now, hold on just a second, that's a bit extreme.'** No, Jesus accepts his worship. He doesn't bat an eyelid. Because Thomas has got it exactly right.

You see, Jesus doesn't say to Thomas or to anyone else – just believe, cross your fingers and keep up some wishful thinking that has no basis in reality. No, he says you are right to want evidence… and here I am.

You decide

In English lessons at school it's important to know the difference between a work of fiction and a work of non-fiction. One is just a made-up story but the other records real facts and is meant to be read as such.

The Bible claims to be a work of non-fiction. It asks us to examine the evidence and to draw our own conclusions. Because Christianity stands or falls on this one historical event: the resurrection of Jesus Christ.

If Jesus really rose from the grave, then we can know God has accepted Jesus' sacrifice on our behalf and that Jesus must be God, just as he claimed to be.

Which leaves us with a decision to make ourselves.

If Jesus did truly rise from the grave then surely we must also accept that everything he said is true. After all, no one has ever done this before or since.

WHAT DO YOU THINK?

What difference would it make to you to see someone come back to life?

What questions do you want to ask Jesus?

What do you think God wants from you?

Emma's story

In the Bible it says, 'Believe in the Lord Jesus, and you will be saved'. Believe that he died on the cross for you and choose to live for him.

WHAT MUST I DO???

The technology for monitoring what you're doing during IT lessons at school has improved somewhat over the years. There was no such technology when I was at school.

The challenge during IT was to sit at a certain computer – because it had a hard drive. Now, I know, I know, as hard as it is to believe today, not all computers used to have hard drives. But this one did. And so, buried deep in some unlikely sounding directory, we had installed a copy of a driving game called E-Type. The challenge was how long you could make it look like you were doing your work whilst secretly playing video games.

Until one week the head of IT informed us that he had been running the virus checking software and noticed some unusual file names being scanned. He didn't know who had hidden the game or where, but he wanted the people responsible to remove it. He wanted a response!

Of course we could have done nothing and left the game there. But we didn't. We knew there would be consequences!

The Bible says that God also wants a response from us. The people who wrote the accounts of Jesus' life did so because they wanted us to respond in a certain way. This is how John puts it at the end of his Gospel.

John 20:30,31

[30] Jesus performed many other signs in the presence of his disciples, which are not recorded in this book. [31] But these are written that you may believe that Jesus is the Messiah, the Son of God, and that by believing you may have life in his name.

God's story

In this book we have been thinking about God's story and looking at several parts of the Bible that speak to us about Jesus.

We began in a manger and saw that because of his great love for us, God himself became a human being. He stepped down from the glory of heaven to be born as a helpless child. He did it in order to be the Saviour that we needed more than anything else.

The love that Jesus had for us took him to the cross where he died in the place of sinful human beings. He was punished in our place. But he did not stay dead and three days later the grave was empty - Jesus was alive.

Now, eternal life is promised to everyone who believes that this is true and puts their faith in Jesus.

Why is this story the most important story of all?

Because it was

'written that you may believe that Jesus is the Messiah, the Son of God, and that by believing you may have life in his name.'

God offers us something we cannot get anywhere else.

He offers us the gift of life as it was always meant to be lived - in relationship with God both now and for eternity.

My story

The thing with gifts is that you are always left with a choice as to what to do with that gift. You can choose to receive the gift with thankfulness or leave it unopened. You can enjoy the gift yourself or try to get rid of it on eBay.

A Christian is simply someone who accepts God's gift of forgiveness and enjoys the relationship with God that this makes possible. Christians believe that God comes to live with us, giving life new direction and meaning.

It was at secondary school that I became a Christian. For me, the overwhelming reason for this was that I simply came to believe that it was all true.

Christianity wasn't just a story for someone else. It wasn't just something that someone had invented to make people feel better. I had this deep sense that it was all wonderfully true.

Becoming a Christian is really a very simple thing. You don't have to wait to feel a certain way or to see God mysteriously write your name in the clouds. Instead, you just have to talk to him. Christians call this prayer.

I don't remember the exact words of the prayer I prayed that night, but I do know it went something like this.

Sorry

God, I'm sorry. I'm sorry for all the things I've done wrong and the ways that I have ignored you in the past. I don't want to live like that any more.

Thank you

Thank you for sending Jesus to die for me. I believe that he died in my place and I trust that he is able to forgive me.

Please

Please help me to live my life with you at the centre and in a way that honours and pleases you. Amen.

It was a very simple prayer, but I meant it with all my heart.

I wish I could say there were bright lights and feelings of great joy. Or that angels showed up singing Handel's *Messiah*. It seemed that nothing had changed very much.

Yet the true story is that everything had changed.

God had forgiven me and
welcomed me into his family. God
had started to change my life.

Rather than worrying about the
future, I knew that God had a plan.

Rather than being concerned as to
what other people thought of me, I
knew God loved me no matter what.

The most important thing in life
was no longer exam results or
image or success, but knowing
God and learning to trust him.

And, in time, God would give me this
amazing opportunity to tell other young
people that the message of Jesus is all
completely true. Which is why I wrote
this book that you're reading now.

So that you would know there is a
God who loves you. Yes, even you.

A God who wants to know you.

A God who sent his Son to die for you.

A God who calls you to
trust Jesus yourself.

Your story

The question, then, is this: how will you respond? How will God's story fit into your story? How will your story fit into God's great story?

Maybe you have questions you'd like to ask - why not start by asking the person who gave you this book? If they're a Christian they would probably love to talk to you about Jesus some more.

If you're able to, why not decide to look into these things some more for yourself? Perhaps there's a church near you where you could go and find out more. Alternatively, if your school has a Christian Union you could start there.

Maybe for some of you, though, you're convinced. As you've read these passages from the Bible you, like many before you, have realised that God is speaking to you. If that's you and you would like to come to know God yourself, then you could pray a prayer similar to the one that I prayed.

God, I'm sorry that I've been living my life without you. I realise that I need your forgiveness. Thank you for sending Jesus to die for me, to take the punishment that I deserve so that I can be forgiven and free. Please help me to live with you and for you from now on. Amen.

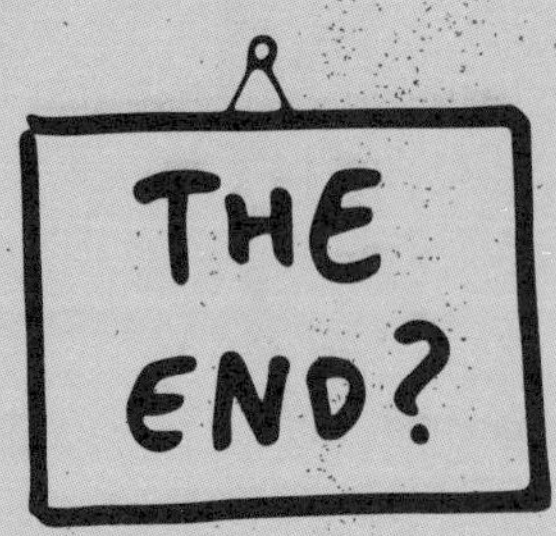